# SEEDS

## Stories of Afro-Indigenous Resilience

Poems and Illustrations
by Dominique Daye Hunter

Cover designed by Dominique Daye Hunter
Illustrated by Dominique Daye Hunter
Edited by K Butterfly Smith, MFA – Directing, CPTT & Founder of KGPLA Mixed Media Cooperative

Printed in the United States of America

D. Daye Hunter Designs acknowledges the O'odham and Piipash communities who are the caretakers of their traditional and ancestral territories where we currently reside. We pay respect to their histories, traditions, and continuous living cultures and commit to respectful relations.

*To the Earth,*
   *to the Water,*
      *to the Fire,*
         *to the Wind,*
            *and to the Seeds.*

"What didn't you do to bury me,
but you forgot that I was a seed."
-Dinos Christianopoulos

# Dear Reader,

Bisé:huk. First, allow me to thank you. Your purchase of this book and support of my storytelling art form, both written and visual, has made my dream of publishing a full-length collection of poetry possible.

The first edition of *Seeds* was published in the fall of 2018. At just 30 pages, the poems in the first edition were truly the seeds which bloomed into this full-length version. I have had the pleasure of sharing pieces from the first *Seeds* to many. Some of those poems from the first edition are present here, and some are not. The original *Seeds* was an accumulation of my best work from 2015 to 2018, but it needed to grow and be refined.

The vital question I asked myself in redefining this book was, "What is the message?" I didn't want another miscellaneous book of poetry. I wanted a collection of works that represented my experiences through the lens of an Afro-Indigenous, neurodivergent woman. Though most pieces come from my personal perspective, I also share stories here which were inspired by my ancestors, family, friends, and historical figures.
The first edition of *Seeds* was about "What will people like? What is palatable?" The book you hold in your hand is much like its author: matured.

I am not the same person I was in 2015. The Dominique who writes these words has learned of her rightful place in this world as a warrior queen. She has learned her worth and has faced rejection and death: figuratively and literally. There were days when I wanted to give up on myself and my dream of being a full-time author and artist. I not only survived, but, having been refined by the flames of adversity, am now thriving unapologetically. This is not despite, but because I am on the autism spectrum and experience chronic health issues like fibromyalgia and stage four endometriosis.

The goal of this book isn't to educate non-Black Indigenous People of Color (BIPOC) on our experiences, though I'm sure that will be one of the byproducts. The reason I wrote this book is to remind our people that we are *resilient*. Storytelling is vital to our survival and existence as Black and Indigenous people. Written literature is the modern-day version of the oral tradition. Both are methods of storytelling. They showcase our ways of being and belonging to land and place, to two and four legged's, and to each other.

Our ancestors have suffered tremendously. Our people still suffer and perish daily from the plague that is colonization. Do not let them die in vain. Continue your healing journey even if it feels like you are going in circles. The spiritual guides honor those who are dedicated to breaking generational curses.

It took me ten plus years, and, though healing is a journey and not a destination, I am humbled and forever grateful to say I don't loathe life anymore. If you can relate to my words, please remember that you are not alone, and healing will come if you are consistent, persistent, and insistent. This is no time to be complacent: we are at war. We've been at war. We've been experiencing genocide for hundreds of years and now the effects of colonization on the Earth have put all our lives in jeopardy: the global majority and non-BIPOC. But we as BIPOC are affected first.

Let these words be the seeds planted into the hearts of our mothers, fathers, parents, and grandparents to heal them. Let these words be the seeds planted into the hearts of our children, and of current and future leaders to guide them. Our survival depends on the harvest that these seeds will bring.

With love and respect,
Dominique

P.S.: There is an Indigenous language glossary in the back of this book. If a word is unfamiliar to you, look there to find deeper meaning.

# Contents

## Maste

Dogwoods are blooming.
Corn seeds wait in aging hands:
full of potential.

## Hazel, Buck, and Rabbit

Short, crunchy footfalls resounded amongst long forgotten leaves of the previous autumn's memory. Their stories became muffled by the fresh overgrowth of the 1950 summer. Three footfalls to be exact: one belonging to Hazel, one belonging to Buck, and one belonging to Rabbit.

All three children were as different as the strong pines, as the red mud, and as the honeybees. Rabbit was her nickname given to her by her father. She was born a triplet, but was the sole survivor. The other two babies passed shortly after being brought into this world. Their tiny graves were adorned with flowers each spring, as all the Cousin's were. Her daddy said she was so small when she was born that she fit in his hand like a little rabbit. So, they nicknamed her Rabbit.

Hazel was a strong independent girl. She was not afraid of defending her siblings or telling it as she saw it, even to an adult. She was the oldest girl of her eleven siblings, and she defended them all like a second mother. Buck was as stubborn and wild as his name indicated.

The three brown Afro-Indigenous children leapt through the chlorophyll filtered sunshine with Hazel in the lead, followed by Buck, and then by Rabbit. With their age gap, Hazel being 13, Buck being 11, and Rabbit being 6 years of age, you wouldn't have guessed that these three would be companions on a mid-summer's day. But their sisters, nicknamed Bones and Rooster, were helping their mother cook and watch the babies. James and June, short for Junior, were grown and out living their own lives while their teen brothers Popcorn and Pancake were helping their father in the fields. So, determined Hazel, headstrong Buck, and inquisitive Rabbit headed off into the forest to get water from the well.

Apart from the chore, there was another reason Hazel offered to pull water. She had a lot on her mind and wanted the time alone to sort it all out. Yet, she was severely disappointed when their father commanded her to take her little brother with her to help. Buck always got on her nerves, especially because he was always fighting with her favorite big brother Pancake.

Rabbit was simply along for the ride, or so everyone thought. She was tired of being lumped in with the little kids. Rabbit often had to help their mother with baby Gwen or get her toddler brother Odie out of a mess. That day Rabbit decided to cut a little slice of her own adventure pie. When she overheard all the talk about going to the well, she popped out from behind the shed to excitedly say, "I'm down!"

-

Hazel had a theory about their family, but Buck had a countertheory.

"What the family needs to do is harvest all the tobacco we can. That way we'll sell enough at market to make it through the winter," Hazel said aloud to herself. She didn't invite Buck into her thoughts, but he interjected anyway.

"Uh-uh, what the family need most is to store up wood for the winter," Buck yelled cutting at the brush with his sling blade. "Also, fewer chores for us kids."

"Well, of course you would say that," scoffed Hazel as she peered through the foliage to look for the well. It would still be in the same place, but the Carolina ivy caused the landscape to take on a new life each year.

"All y'all kids want is to get out of chores and gripe about caring for the babies. While us grown folk gotta worry about our food crop and getting jobs if the tobacco harvest ain't big enough."

"Ha!" Buck retorted, "You ain't grown. You barely older than me."

Hazel rolled her eyes, ignoring him. "Pancake said last time he tried to go into town to get a job they said they ain't hiring colored folks. So, we gotta work extra hard."

"We ain't gonna go hungry," Buck replied shortly, "Daddy sure as nothing gone let us go hungry."
Rabbit said, "Mmhmm!" in agreement.

"Besides," continued Buck lackadaisically, "If we don't grow enough tobacco this year, we'll survive off the land!"

Hazel turned red and got a stern look on her face. What did her little brother know about anything? He was always horsing around. It was her job to keep them all together. To keep them safe. Rabbit hid behind her brother while Hazel stormed past them down the path to the well.

-

After they fetched the water, Buck took a break to lean on a tree. Hazel was still pacing back and forth, her brow furrowed in deep thought. She was so stuck in her own head that she tripped over a tree branch and fell face first in the mud.

4

Buck cracked up laughing, "Those shoes must be comfortable, 'cause they don't work and they sure are ugly!"

"Oh, aren't you a common comedian?!" Hazel snapped before narrowing her eyes on something near her brother's feet.

"What are those?" she said as she scrunched her face up and squinted her eyes to focus.
"What's what?!" he replied spinning around.
"They seedlings!" Rabbit said squatting down and pointing to the small tobacco plants that had sprouted up.
"Hey! If we don't harvest enough on our fields, we can harvest some of these, too!" Buck said excitedly.
"Ha! They'll be dead come October!" said Hazel.
"No, they won't!" Buck retorted defensively, "And ya gonna save our family farm. Ain't cha?" he asked the sprouts tenderly.
"How they gonna grow if no one's tending to 'em?!" Hazel said indignantly.
"They doing just fine now! Them seeds is strong. Blew in all the way from the fields and planted themselves. How do ya like that?!" he shouted angrily.

Then Hazel shoved her brother causing him to fall onto the patch of seedlings. She was only a couple years older than him, but she was tall and strong as a bull.

He hollered loud enough for the birds in Tampa to hear him. "What in the hell did ya do that for?!" he asked, shoving her into a nearby tree and grasping at his ripped pants. "Now I'm-a get whooped for tearing up my clothes!"
"And ya got mud all over mine! When Daddy finds out he's gone whoop ya hide, and he's gone whoop mine, too!" she said wiping her tears away. She looked up and saw

tears in her brother's eyes, too. He quickly looked up so they would disappear, unlike the fear of their father that stayed with him, stayed with them both, stayed with them all.

By this time even Rabbit was sniffling with tears and snot running down her face as her lip quivered. She tried to wipe it away on her dress sleeve and left a long trail of slimy residue.

"Now mama's gone whoop me for crying all over my dress," she said glancing at the snot stain.

"Yeah, we all gone get whooped," Buck said examining their badly stained clothes.

Rabbit dried her eyes on her other sleeve and did something neither of them expected. She was quiet, but observant and had grown tired of their bellyaching. So, she spoke up.

"We goin' to the lake!" she demanded. Only five simple words, yet Rabbit had never told them what to do. Hazel and Buck were shocked. They stood with mouths wide open in disbelief. They were both still too proud to speak to each other. So, they gave each other a mean look, and followed their little sister to the lake.

-

Buck stood on the shoreline and threw stones as Rabbit played in the sand. Hazel searched for seashells and stones; and picked up a shell that was roughly the shape of a Dogwood flower. She smiled remembering her grandmama telling her stories about waiting for the Dogwoods to bloom before planting corn.

She remembered the cold spring mornings spent with her planting the seeds, followed by warmer afternoons learning to make quilts, and late summer harvests sucking on ears of sweet white corn, followed by autumn days grinding up yellow and red corn to store for cornbread and grits in the winter months. She closed her eyes and hugged the memories close to her like a dear friend, only to open her eyes and see her annoying little brother.

She never understood why they grew tobacco. Granddaddy didn't speak much, but he would talk from time to time about it being a sacred plant passed down from their "Indian" ancestors. Daddy spoke even less, and just said "'Cause I said so." He would go to the Johnson's and trade some of the family corn for their corn whiskey. When he left the house, she always feared he'd come back drunk and mean as a snake.

She knew the corn made him drunk, but the smell of the tobacco in his old wooden pipe is what haunted her. She gagged thinking about it. But since tobacco sold for a lot at market and was good for the family Hazel had to put her own feelings aside.

Buck walked up to her and spoke, "Ya know, maybe we won't grow enough tobacco."

She picked up a rock: flat and smooth. Without looking at him, she skipped the rock along the lake surface. "Yeah, and maybe we will."

They sat in silence for a while.

"Well, we better head on back," Hazel said finally breaking the silence, "It's almost sundown and if we ain't back before nightfall we gone get two whoopings." They both laughed.

"C'mon, Rabbit," Buck called out to his little sister.

"Aww, man!" Rabbit whined.

"Hey, now. No hollering or else I'll whoop ya, too! C'mon," he said as he approached her. She stood and lifted her hands up. He shook his head as if to say, "Ya ain't a baby no more. Plus, I'm carrying all this water." But the look in her big brown eyes, especially after she wiped the sleepiness from them, hit his tender spot.

"Maybe tomorrow, 'kay? C'mon now."

He lifted the buckets over his shoulders, and they headed into the woods followed by Hazel. They walked back to the farm, back to their home, back to the land where the Dogwoods, the tobacco, the corn, and their people grow.

## Grounded

I step outside
to heal my soul,
and cry
with the Earth.

Á:tʰi Mạ:tọ́: rain
heals my pain,
and brings about
new birth.

I sit with flowers,
and talk for hours
like catching up
with sisters.

I'll hold these moments
within my wasu:ti
and yạ:di
for many, many winters.

## Our Resilience, Our Identity, Our Pride

We are the Afro diaspora:
from Ghana to Alabama,
from Onodaga to Diné tah,
from Cochiti to Saponi to Mvskoke.

We are the originators
of the twerk, the juke,
and of viral moves.

Rock and roll, Soul, and the Blues,
all have Afro-Indigenous roots.
Corn bread, hominy grits, and barbecue, too.

We are the creators of the modern hairbrush
and of shampoo headrests at salons.
We patented the hair straightener
and that cellular phone that you stay on.

"Go awf, sis!"
"Understood the assignment,"
and "Yaaaaas, QUEEN":
these all came from we.

Our crowns of tresses range from 2b to 4c.
We come in all shades of beauty
from "Sand" and "Honey"
to "Nutmeg" and "Ebony."
Despite colonization,
we raise hands for praying,
and wear jingle dresses for healing.

We face anti-Blackness
at work and, unfortunately,
in our own communities.

Yet, we persist to exist
unapologetically.

We're returning home
both within Turtle Island
and to the Mother Land.

We are
as brilliant as the stars,
as transformative as the Moon,
as immovable as the Sun.
We rise.
We stand.
We overcome.

## Never Say Never

I've never felt more pain.
I've never felt more beautiful.
I've never felt more powerful.
I've never felt more alive.

These circumstances aren't happening to me.
These circumstances are happening for me.

I've never felt so divine.

## Hold On

Hold on to what is good
even if it's a handful of Earth.
Hold on to what you believe,
even if, like a tree, you stand by yourself.
Hold on to what you must do,
even if it's a long way from here.
Hold on to your life,
even if it's easier to let go.

## Addicted to Chaos

I am pulled into you once again:
drawn in...
pulled in...
Promises and dreams were so memorialized.
Will they ever be realized?
Or am I a moth to a flame?
How do I tell my good hopes from a manic demise?
How do I differentiate
goals from an armored disguise
designed to please others,
covered in holes of insecurity?
"I'll never leave you if you don't leave me
like ma and dad did when I was a kid."
Why do we crave those who hurt us?
Why, after all the destruction,
are we still addicted to chaos?

## Change

I cry my eyes out
knowing I shared my heart
with someone who hates my light,
because it shows their own darkness.
I look over to see
a photograph of my grandmother.
She looks beautiful yet sad.
The weight of trauma
shows through her eyes.
Her eyes are like mine.
Those sad eyes ask,
"Why do you ignore me?
Why do you beat me?
Why do you hang me?
Am I not a queen?
Am I not the foundation of the world?
Am I not the cornerstone for life?
Why am I treated like trash?
Why does no one care for me?
Am I worthless?
Unloveable?
No.
But I am certainly treated as such."

The painful weight
of being a Black Indigenous queer woman
which is passed down from generation to generation
like heavy wool in August,
like shoeless, haunting winters.
We walk through the snow.
We wade in the water.
We buckle under the weight of the ocean
as it collapses our lungs.
We hear the lewd laughter

as they trespass our bodies.
We feel the weight:
it's all around us.
It surrounds us.
It crushes us
as we sink
under the weight.
It. is. too. heavy.

Beasts of burden
fated to carry
the insecurity
of white people's internal darkness
upon our ebony skin.
"It matches," they declare.
But the darkest tones come
from sitting in the sun-lit air.
We are dark because we
absorb the light
not shy away from it.
But this is not as much about color
as about culture.
We love light.
We can't help it.
But we live in a seemingly
endless, colonial winter:
the cold suppressing life indefinitely.

I finish typing my college paper
between mental breakdowns
while trying to deprogram myself
from abuse and lies.
I'm living on the brink of death
trying to do all the right things,
but still feeling all the wrong ways.
I'm not drinking,

but I'm still over-thinking.
I'm not popping pills,
but I'm still popping off
and pushing people away.
I'm trying to stay true to myself
while desperately needing a kind ear
hoping that one day I'll heal,
hoping that one day
things will change.

## Lightning

I'm quick like the lightning as it strikes the Earth.
I'm quick like my addiction spiraling,
like my mind unraveling.
I'm slow to judge and quick to forgive,
and if you ask me what happened,
I may only remember the wrong I did.
I'm quick to show love
while refracting it away from myself.
I'm quick to assist others,
but slow regarding my own mental health.
I'm slow to assess missing cards that weren't dealt.
I'm quick to make Kings out of Jokers,
and black hearts
into shimmering diamonds
that are carefully remolded and set higher
than celestial royalty
in an attempt to display the refined illusion
of this queen's gracious glory.
I'm quick to make myself useful,
quick to think I am useless.
I'm quick to say I'm over it,
quick to resubmit to the nonsense
I'm quick like the lightning as it strikes the Earth.
But the collateral is all mine,
for what it's worth.

## Park Plans

I sit on this bench
where we once sat
on that warm summer night.
The park lights were bright,
but the mood was far from light.
We talked of our pasts,
and planned our future.
I sighed and looked down,
"Will I be a good mom?
or will I be like…her?"

As I sit here with them,
these borrowed children,
it's clear:
the future is bright.

## Lost Voices, Part 1

When I explain my life
and hardships as a
Black Native woman
most don't understand
unless they've walked in my shoes,
or they've put down their pride and listened.
Listen to my stories:
our stories,
the stories of my own life
and those my ancestors carried.
Generation after generation,
their backs broken
under the weight they carried.
The connection between
inter-generational trauma
and destiny.

## Lost Voices, Part 2

I walk the narrow path.
I walk the Red Road.
I walk in the footsteps
of a Black woman,
of a Native woman:
one and the same.

The everyday struggle,
problems left for the next generation.
Pitfalls with sinking foundations set before birth.
This can't be the extent of our inheritance:
bloody, bare footprints.
We are more than this:
more than cheap Halloween costumes
and stereotypical images.
We deserve more than an excuse mockingly offered
by a sick, broken man:
"She put herself in that situation."
"They asked for it."

We are lovable.
We are beautiful.
We are valuable.
We are powerful.
Yet, to heal
there needs to be real
recognition
that we are suffering,
and that we are hurting.

When we fall,
with injustice and inequality,
they laugh at us.
When we told them of our mental-illness

and subjugated status,
they summed us up as:
"Just another drunk 'Indian,'"
"Just another crazy Black woman,"
raising "criminal children."

We have some support
from our communities,
but many of our people
are going through
their own trials and tragedies.
Many times, we look for help
within our families
that are still dysfunctional.
So, we look above
for Their wisdom and Their guidance
to heal our intergenerational traumas.
We share our pain,
but colonizers hear complaints.
We go missing and no one goes searching.
Our own people are so numb from all the loss
that they, that we, have suffered
for hundreds of years.
Some can only sigh when we die:
they can't even cry.
They can't even cry.

We can't excuse this any longer.
We must be stronger.
We must live up
to the path of our ancestors,
for our children,
our sons, and our daughters.
We must stand up.
Our voices will be heard.
We will not stop.

We will not stay silent.
We will only get louder!
We will be a voice for the voiceless
through all Their help and Their power.
All my relations:
saving our people,
the heart of our Nations,
one voice at a time.

## Divergence of Domestic Dwellings

Columns of cedar rise to rooftops.
The beams are so different from the plaster
that, as a child, kept me prisoner.
Perhaps they are only so different
because of my personal experience.
One person's paradise is another's hell.

I'm learning that I don't need to suffer
to earn my peace of mind.
I'm learning that the key to healing is not
needlessly prodding at my own pain.

# A Tangled Mind Is a Terrible Thing to Waste

I feel like I'm crazy
banging my head against the wall,
because you're no longer my baby.
There's been too much change going on,
and too much pain. I feel anxious.
No, anxiety would be an understatement.
I feel like I want to crawl out of my skin
or crawl to the bottle: pills or gin.
I can't focus on anything long enough
without feeling the weight of a tidal wave
crashing in and down around me.
I can't focus through the static long enough
to see if or when I'll ever be happy.
I lash out with a frustrated shout,
because I still don't know what this is all about.
I'm still not sure if you're like the monstrous mother from
my childhood.
If I simply had more time


and space


to think......... and grace
to be me
perhaps life wouldn't be
as difficult as I think it needs to be.

I let out a breath.
At long last I see the mess before me
like tangle vines searching for light.
I take a step back and see a garden:
I realize the garden is my mind.
I was so caught up in the thicket and the weeds

that I couldn't see the proverbial forest for the trees.
I allowed the voices that are discouraging
to ring far too loudly.
I hear the voices still, but as an echo
rather than as a loud bell ringing
and pounding within my ear drums.
"You are strange."
"You are weird."
"You are other."
"You do not belong."
"You are disliked."
"You are alien."
"You are other."
"You are wrong."

Just when I'm tempted to listen
to these voices once again,
which I've realized are mostly the ghosts of
people from my past,
and some from the present,
I hear something more beautiful
that catches my attention:
a thud. thud. thud. thud.
My heart beat.

I hear another:
a wisp. wisp. wisp. wisp.
My breathing.

And yet another:
a mumble. mumble. mumble. mumble.
My mind speaking
to itself.

These voices grow more powerful
than those that are opposing.

I look back at the tangled mess
and see now that it's glowing.
Rather than tangled, I see that it's highly connected
and receptive of itself.
I can hear it laughing joyfully
as it discovers new things.
It sees patterns and mimics them to learn.
It makes the whole garden come to life.
They all rejoice to see it smile:
a warm pink glow amongst black rich earth
with sparks of inspiration like stars stretched
over the vast universe.
The voices get closer
and then become more in sync
until I can almost make out what it is saying.
I gasp in near disbelief:
this thing I've discovered
is the most beautiful creature I've ever seen.
I see her now so clearly:
**she is me.**

## Imperfectly Me

I'm sick and tired of being treated differently
when I'm showing all of me.
Neurodivergence is by nature
different,
hence the suffix "divergent."
Yes, we are different:
Autism, dyspraxia,
dyslexia, dyscalculia,
OCD, ADHD
to name a few.
These labels can help or hurt us
depending on whether they
describe who we are
or simply what we tend to do
as "different."
Yes, being neurodivergent
inherently makes us unique.
But we are not alone or unique in our uniqueness.
We are not more, and we are certainly not less.

Even with no labels attached,
when we exist without our "masks"
of "normalcy"
we are viewed as "freaks":
freaks who are too excited about certain topics,
"weirdos" who don't always catch onto
social cues and taboos,
outsiders who are "other than,"
because the lights are too bright,
the books on the shelf are not aligned just right,
because the music is too loud or not loud enough,
because we don't have enough space to be ourselves.

So, the next time I talk about astrology

or comic books or my process of self-discovery
long past your point of interest,
please indulge me
long enough and then politely change the subject.
Next time I trip and spill my drink
all over myself at a dinner party
do not mock me
for I oft pull more accomplishments
out of thin air
than most people pull excuses out of their asses.
Next time I do something "weird"
instead of making the situation
more "awkward,"
please cover me with a love
that doesn't always need
to understand in that moment.
Next time that I am simply being me,
remember that I am not inherently "wrong."
Acceptance at best or, at a minimum, indifference,
is what I've wanted all along.
But I'm okay with myself
if you still think I'm a freak.
Because I accept and love all of me:
inherently, neurodivergently, imperfectly me.

## Nothing Like Reality

Plastic shoes on concrete are
nothing like mud between my feet.
Fueling my car with dead oil is
nothing like the sound of hooves against soil.

All human inventions of aviation are
nothing like winged ones of various nations.
Trading currency for groceries is
nothing like smelling crops fresh and sweet.

Eating animals tortured in pain is
nothing like her sacrifice so that I may sustain.
Being awake late nights watching blue screens is
nothing like sitting beneath galaxies.

The predictable and sedentary life is
nothing like moving and feeling alive.
Watching others' lives on media is
nothing like actually seeing ya.

Wanting materialistic items
which I will never attain is
nothing like the peace which will remain.
Enduring a world so far from reality is
nothing like living, finally free.

## Storms

I didn't realize
you were naive enough
to think that
all that glitters is gold.
Even diamonds were coal.
You see my darkness,
and now you're cold.

We all have darkness.
We need it to balance the light.
My anger isn't a show
for performances or protests.
This rage is real.
You resent how I feel.
I'm turning down the flames
just enough not to burn myself.
But you want someone perfect.
My mama always warned me
about fairy tales and Disney princesses
who need to be saved.
She said, "You gotta be independent and brave."
I guess you weren't taught the same.

Now we're at a crossroads.
I don't remember how we got here though.
Everything was going great
then you yelled in my face.
You told me to suck it up,
but it's depression not a phase!
You saw my glory days,
but for storms will you stay?
Every time it thunders you walk away,
but we grow from rain.
Even dirt nurtures sage.

It blesses you as you pray.
You wanted my beauty,
but not the growing pains.
I guess I'm partly to blame:
as a child of alcoholics
I always dreamed of being perfect.
I lied to myself, and I was lied to.
I guess they lied to you, too.

## Star Blanket Visions

Under a thousand stars,
under a thousand hides,
under a thousand feathers,
under a thousand trees,
under a thousand souls,
under a thousand teeth:
all spinning.

## Poor NDN Love

Greasy yet tasty.
Humble yet sustaining.
Indigent yet still proudly
Indigenous.
The poor NDN's grub:
just like poor NDN love.
"It's so simple,
but most want to complicate it,
offering articulated
actions and words that are manipulated
to gain control
and gain attachment."
"You should be your own shoulder to cry on,
your own best friend.
Stand up for yourself and walk on those two legs!"
He said,
"It's simple you see:
the best things to love are freed."

## In the Darkness

I realize now that you never loved or liked me.
You were infatuated with me.
But now I understand it as
the lust of control and disgust.
My existence is a threat to yours.
My kindness intrigues and enrages you
because it shows so clearly
how hateful
and how selfish
and how miserable you are.

I realize now that you never cared for me.
You simply needed me.
You needed the proximity to me so badly
for your own selfish gains
and to keep access to me
so that you could slowly yet surely
transition from loving to indifferent
and from indifference to blatant neglect.
You tricked me into believing I
no longer and never deserved respect.

I realize now that you dislike me.
You hate me really,
because I am everything you are not
and everything you can never be.
My light shows how long
your shadow does stretch.
You want to snuff me out.

Foolish, hateful boy,
snake in the grass
full of insecurities
waiting for an impossibility:

the downfall of this Queen
at the hands of a charlatan
upon whom even bottom feeders
wouldn't feed.

Haven't you noticed?
The harder you try,
the brighter I shine
in the darkness.

## Summer

The days get hotter,
humid with bright foliage
as we hold our dreams tightly.

## Abalone

I am like abalone:
humble yet radiant,
earthy yet colorful,
filled with holes yet whole,
and I shine most when
I am prayed over.
I am an eternal reflection
of the universe's beauty.

## Soaring

I soar towards the Earth on the wings of twilight.
"Kihó:, daughter," she says,
"Come back to us."

I fly on metal wings, seeing green and ancient trees.
"Kihó:, daughter," they say,
"Come back to us."

I sit next to strangers, but I hear ancestors.
"Kihó:, daughter," they say,
"Come back to us."

I greet the rain droplets in the clouds, mixed with my own
tears now.
"Kihó:, daughter," they say,
"Come back to us."

The Moon rises on the east, always watching over me,
beaming.
"Here comes our daughter," she says,
"I've brought her back to us."

## Mị

Sitting in the sky,
I see evidence of
how the Sun likes to spend his evenings
with relatives in Sonora,
with relatives in O'odham jeved.
He promises, without words,
that he'll return once again
to visit with us
for morning coffee
here in Akụ:čuk.

## Red Earth Woman

Yesáh mahé:.
Red Earth Woman.
Daughter of the Earth.
Child of the Sun.
We will always be,
always be One.

## Missin' You

I leave the porch light on every night
in case ya come home, but it's alright.
I know ya left long ago to ease the pain,
but I can't let it go. I tried: it's vain.
I know in my heart this love is true.
So, I keep holdin' on missin' you.
Yeah, the love's all here, but I'm missin' you.

So, won't ya come home baby.
Come home soon.
I know ya said there's lots to do.
Ya gotta heal your heart and I'm healin' mine, too.
But remember I'm still here missin' you.
Yeah, I'm here right now missin' you.

Every time I hear George Jones I cry.
Then, I gotta laugh and wonder why
the sweetest love can hurt the most.
'Cause most times it feels like I'm chasin' ghosts.
Yeah, sometimes I feel like I'm chasin' your ghost.

So, won't ya come home baby.
Come home soon.
I know ya said there's lots to do.
Ya gotta heal your heart and I'll heal mine, too.
But remember I'm still here missin' you.
Yeah, remember I'm here missin' you.

Most nights I fall asleep on the couch,
'cause the bed's too cold while you're out.
And when the wind blows, I hear your voice
callin' out to me, "You're my first choice.
Ya know I love you baby. You're my first choice."

So, ya gotta come home baby.
Come home soon.
Get it done quick, 'cause there's lots to do.
I see us old together when the Moon is blue.
So, please remember I'm still here missin' you.
Yeah, I'll always be here missin' you.

## Good Woman

I was heartbroken in the night.
You came along and made me feel alright.
You gave me food and shelter when I was cold,
but every day with you I got older.

I was a good woman.
I was a good woman.
I was a good woman.
But never your woman.

You called me baby 'til one day
you said you didn't love me that-a-way.
I found her messages on your phone.
"She was a friend," you said, but now you're gone.

I was a good woman.
I was a good woman.
I was a good woman.
But never your woman.

Yesterday you called me out the blue.
You said, "Baby, I'm still in love with you."
But I know there's always another,
and now I'm someone else's true lover.

I was a good woman.
I was a good woman.
I was a good woman.
Now, I'm my own woman.

## Cycles

Flowers flowering,
rivers ribboning,
trees trailing
along mountain kin's traversing.
Pinnacle peaks
for fearless fortitude,
for waiting women,
for chanting children.
Waiting forever and not at all,
for the rain to fall,
for Creator's call,
for the sky to ignite
into a ring of fire:
engulfing the sea and granting desire.
Death and life
recycled there
right before her eyes.

## Sacred Ways, Sacred Day

Mother Earth in her most awe-striking complexities
evokes such strong and good memories.
She reminds me that I, too,
shall be reconnected to you
in another small yet sure way
in the thick emerald forest.
Beauty into infinity.
Molecules to galaxies.
Each drop of rain is as precious
as each star that you see.
Foundation of humanity.
So grateful to simply breathe.
Each step is an exchange of ancient
Earth power vibration:
the strength of our relatives
to heal the nations.
It is your choice to live these sacred ways.
So, rise in beauty and live this sacred day

## Spirits Calling

Spirits calling.
Children turning, running
to follow in the footsteps
of grandmothers past.
Words ringing,
truth sinking.
Worlds away they're dreaming:
listening
to the teachings
of the old ones.
Old ways returning,
relearning, rebirthing.
Identity:
centered in molecules of galaxies.
Humbly returning
to the truth within:
the center of all things.

## Ancestral Voice

Each dream that I dream,
each prophecy that is given,
each premonition that is received:
Are the ancestors speaking through me?

Each idea that surfaces,
each inspiration lent,
each creative thought that I think:
Are the ancestors speaking through me?

Each letter I press,
each word I type,
each sentence I complete:
Are the ancestors speaking through me?

Each divine word that I speak,
each mountain that I climb,
each new day that I see:
Are the ancestors speaking through me?

## Maroon

In the jungle lies a legend
of a deep-hued people
who were forced to a new land,
but found refuge amongst equals.

In the swamp lies a truth
of one people born of mutual assistance,
of revolution, of loyalty,
of love, and of resilience.

In the towns they called them "Maroon",
but they call themselves by their own Native names:
Native to Africa, Native to America.
One people, two heritages: one and the same.

In the trees they fought
the original guerrilla warfare
led by Nganga Nzumbi of Quilombo dos Palamares,
led by Cudjoe of Nanny Town Jamaica,
led by Wild Cat and Osceola in Florida.
They are called Palenquero, Quilombola,
Seminole, and Kalunga.

In the jungle lies a legend.
Yes, legendary refugees
who grew from seeds brought
in cornrows of hair across the sea,
and from these seeds their stories
stay tucked beneath tree canopies.


*In honor of the various "Maroon" tribes in Florida, Central America,
and South America.*

## Okay, white man

white man say, "Negroes are our property.
Return them promptly
or face violence and penalty."
Nanticoke *said*, "Okay, white man,"
but laughed to theyselves like a joke.

white man say, "Negroes are our property.
Return them by this date
or there will be murder, pillage, and r*pe.
Delaware *said*, "Okay, white man."
but laughed to theyselves and said, "No."

white man say, "Negroes are little more than animals.
Surrender them now
or we'll come and get them ourselves."
Seminole said, "Never, white man.
Come to the swamp and try it."

white man say, "Negroes are ours to own.
Surrender them now
or we'll come for your home."
Yamasee said, "Never, white man."
Then, started up they own riot.
The white man demanded other tribes do the same.
Like the Iroquois Confederacy,
Huron, Gingaskin, Saponi,
Natchez tribe, and Mattaponi.

They all say the same thing in different ways:
"We ain't giving you our relatives.
They free people now.
They no longer your 'slaves.'"

# Wildfire

A Wildfire was born on July 4th,
and no, I'm not referring to U.S.
Independence from British rule.
I'm referring to the low-rolling fire of 1844
who was Mary Edmonia Lewis:
the Afro-Indigenous artist
they don't teach you about in school.

"Wildfire" was her Indigenous name
and Edmonia was her English.
She was born to an African man
and Ojibwe woman
though she wasn't raised by her parents.

Her mother died when she was three,
and, of her father there isn't much mention.
But her mother made her aunties promise
that they'd raise her in Ojibwe traditions.

Wildfire grew and played
along New York mountain ranges and riverbanks.
Spiritual principles of life were instilled
by her aunties who taught her ancestral craft skills.

At 16, she left for Oberlin College
with the help of her brother
to honor the artistic soul of her mother,
and to honor the creative genius within her.

She was a target of a hate crime beating
and accused of poisoning two white "friends."
She won the appeal
but was later accused of stealing.
Wildfire never graduated.

A victim of racism and segregation.

Nevertheless, she moved to Boston
to open an art studio of her own.
She met abolitionists whose busts she sculpted,
and later found opportunity in Rome.

She was the first Black and first Afro-Indigenous world
renown sculptor
even if most of her works have been lost,
and most history books have omitted her.
She remains a beacon of Black Native excellence and hope,
a spark of creative genius.
As long as we remember her name,
we'll feel the heat from her fire among us.

## Lucy Gonzales Parsons

In 1851, the Seed of Resistance
was born into her human skin:
Lucy Gonzalez Parsons.
Black, Hispanic, and Indigenous:
her parents called her Lucy Gonzalez Parsons.

Once enslaved in Virginia then freed in Texas,
she went by Lucy Gonzalez Parsons.
After marrying a white ally journalist,
she fled for her life to Chicago,
but remained Lucy Gonzalez Parsons.

People of color were captured and murdered,
and her husband was executed
all before the eyes of Lucy Gonzalez Parsons.
From 1887 to 1942, she fought racial injustice.
Her name was Lucy Gonzalez Parsons.

She created the sit-in and non-violent protest.
Say her name! Lucy Gonzalez Parsons!
They gave MLK, Cesar Chavez, and Gandi the credit, but
we remember her name:
Lucy Gonzalez Parsons.

## We Became One People

They said, "Their mixing is to be prevented."
Nevertheless,
we gathered on the open Oklahoma plains.
We married in the deep Minnesota snows.
We became Afro-Indigenous.
We became one people.

They said, "Between the races
we cannot dig too deep a gulf."
Nevertheless,
we fought together in Florida swampland,
we stood with Guerro against injustice in Mexico.
We became Afro-Indigenous.
We became one people.

We saw each other as the same
through the fingerprint called "human being,"
and through the lens of struggle
in Pueblo plazas, in Carolina forests,
in Brazilian jungles.
We became Afro-Indigenous.
We are one people.

# The Battle of Hayes Pond

## 1864 to 1874

The Home Guard said
the Lowry Gang was criminals.
But to us they're Lumbee heroes.
white men kept tying their mules
to our fence posts
and sued us saying we stole 'em,
so they could take our farms and
force us into labor for Confederates
and land stealing racists.

The Guard kept harassing and killing us.
One day we says, "Enough is enough."
Henry Lowry and his boys
started up their raidin.' And then
they started trackin' and huntin'
and killin' Police Guards and sheriffs
and even klan's men.
Eventually, they shot up the Lowry's.
Henry fled and was never seen from again.

## 1958

84 years later, the klan tried
coming back to Lumbee land.
But this time, we had history,
experience, and other tribes with us.
They burned crosses on our lawns
'cause of "racial intermixing."
5 days later,
on the night of January 18, 1958,
in a brisk, dark field in Robeson County
they came with hoods, a microphone,

and a single light bulb.
One hundred white boys
not knowing who surrounded them
in these Maxton woods.
Some say hundreds,
some say a thousand,
American Indians in leather jackets,
wearing Veterans caps and badges,
arms in hand ready to fire.
The Sherriff, Police, even the FBI
tried to stop the rally.
But Cole got on his microphone anyway.
Boy, did he regret it.
American Indians
from all over North Carolina,
charged in on 'em:
They stabbed a hole
in that little light bulb.
All hell broke loose.
Saponi's with baseball bats
they used back in Granville County
to bash up klan's men's mailboxes.
Lumbee's with shot guns
ready to whoop their asses.
Them klan boys ran off like squealing hogs
back to South Carolina,
and never did try that shit again.
That's what happens when the klan
tries to set up shop on Lumbee land.

*In honor of the Lumbee Tribe and Native Americans from various
nations who actively fought white supremacy during the Antebellum
Period, the Reconstruction Era, and the Jim Crow South.*

## I Imagine

I imagine a world without lines
where being Black and Indigenous isn't scoffed at,
isn't a social crime;
where the falsely accused are free,
where treaties mean something,
where children don't have to run and hide
from those who are supposed to protect them,
where Chief Mahenip and Claudette Colvin are national
heroes,
where my Native people don't go missing
without police officers and politicians investigating,
where I don't have to worry about my nephews
walking down the street
because they're wearing a hoodie
and the melanin in their skin is deep.
A world where young persons
don't have to raise their children
without someone to help them.
I imagine…
I imagine a world where we are free
to enjoy the beauty of our diversity.

## Rising

She walks towards the Moon to quiet her soul.
She reaches for darkness to brighten the glow.
Inner light travels to places unknown
from prayers: the weight that anchors this flow.
She searches for insight towards limitless growth.
Lunar light gently warms the Earthen womb
as it grows and grows and grows...

## A Prayer to Maní

Maní, humbly I ask,
with guidance from your reflective light:
carry me into this life

Maní, humbly I ask,
with protection from the river's currents:
carry my boat and my heavy burdens.

Maní, humbly I ask,
with healing from the wind and rain:
carry the tears that heal my pain.

Maní, humbly I ask,
with showers from clouds so high:
carry our crops born of Earth and Sky.

Maní, humbly I ask,
with the watchfulness of a midwife:
carry my child into the light.

Maní, humbly I ask,
with your guidance to return:
carry my soul into the next world

# Black

Black like slate stone:
sturdy and smooth.

Black like burnt bones:
straight and true.

Black like bear prints:
trusted and safe.

Black like obsidian arrowheads:
sharpened and shaved.

Black like Raven's wings:
wise and blessed.

Black like snake tracks:
medicine for flesh.

Black like moonless nights:
medicine for crystals and plants.

Black like the womb:
quiet for planning.

Black like the starlit sky:
festive for birthing.
Black like swamp mud:
teaming with life.

Black like domestic felines:
powerful friends.

Black like thick hair:
enduring and mysterious.

Black like onyx:
a shield and a healer.

Blacklisted books:
full of magic and history.

Black like deep skin:
full of love and divinity.

## Don't Tell the Neighbors

Don't tell the neighbors that mama burns
the hair she sheds:
they'll call the patty wagon and drag her away.

Don't tell the neighbors that sister changes light switches
with her eyes, with her mind.

Don't tell the neighbors about your tremors:
how sometimes you hear the voices of our ancestors.

Don't tell the neighbors that grandmama has eyes in the
back of her head:
she saw you roll your eyes at her after she turned away
from you,
and whooped your behind because of it.

Don't tell the neighbors that the only sickness that lingers
here is the sickness of sadness
that flows out of mama's heart because she takes on all our
pain.

Don't tell the neighbors how she's always filled up with
liquid spirits that make her laugh and help her forget the
past, at least for a little while.

## Wild

"Wild. Untamed," they say.
I don't see what they see.
I simply see me totally free,
and a crown of hair
that's proud to be.

"Wild. Untamed," they say.
So, I put you away
for a rainy day.
I'll bring you out again
I promise
…one day.

"Wild. Untamed," they say.
Promises turn to reasons,
reasons turn to seasons
of relaxers, creams, wigs, and
dreams of what a perfect
you would be.

"Wild. Untamed," they say.
Now I believe them,
because I'm fed up with you, too.
Whatever I do
you do the opposite.
I want you curly: you're flat and straight
I want you calm: you're enraged
with beauty and in pain.

"Wild. Untamed," they say.
So, I tuck you away
and walk away from the mirror
and the shame which I feel more clearly than
what my two eyes can see.

My third eye cries.

"Wild. Untamed," they say.
"Fuck it!" I reply.
I look to the sky and give thanks.
I look within and sing praise,
because within your tresses are
DNA memory
older than European standards of beauty
which are anything but original.

"Wild. Untamed," they say.
I reply, "Say it louder!
She loves that I've found her!"
They tried to bury you,
cut you, and silence you.
But I will carry you,
the dear crown of my ancestors:
blended and blessed.
I will give you back your voice.
With each strand there's a choice:
I choose love and acceptance.
After all, that's all we both
ever wanted.

# How to Survive as a Writer

I sigh. I love writing, but I hate deadlines.
They make me feel like I'm pimping out my mind:
a sell-out slanging forced insights and lies.

Why is it so difficult to think
creatively after weeks of
thinking objectively?
I answer my own question:
"Creative mental apathy."

Overworking my mind leads to lethargy,
nights without sleep,
days without peace,
and a headache, at the least.

I need a damn break
from minutes and clients,
from appointments and protein shakes.
I need a hot, fresh meal
made with love and a few tears.
I need to be stripped of ego,
and relieved of responsibility,
at least momentarily.
My mind needs to be led
into a safe space for learning,
not tricked into churning
and producing and maximizing.
Oh, it's exhausting!

But I cannot deny that a deadline
lovingly, sternly forces me to write.

## With Each Step

With each swing she readies the ground,
she readies the ground,
she readies the ground,
she readies the ground.

With each finger she pushes seeds down,
she pushes them down,
she pushes them down,
she pushes them down.

With each breath she begins to pray,
she begins to pray,
she begins to pray,
she begins to pray.

With each word she calls out for rain,
she calls out for rain,
she calls out for rain,
she calls out for rain.

With each step she heals all their pain,
she heals all their pain,
she heals all their pain,
she heals all their pain.


With each tear she waters her seeds,
she waters her seeds,
she waters her seeds,
she waters her seeds.

With each day she wakes and believes,
she wakes and believes,
she wakes and believes,

she wakes and believes.

With each struggle she keeps her hope,
she keeps her hope,
she keeps her hope,
she keeps her hope.

With each blessing she is thankful,
she is thankful,
she is thankful,
she is thankful.

## Hot, Cold, Strong

Aka:t$^h$eka like sparks, like summer, like sweat.
Aka:t$^h$ekawa: like the furnace, like this season, like my flesh.
Aka:t$^h$ekase: like my anger, like my fever, like my stress.
Aka:t$^h$ekala: like our fires, like our passion, like our finesse.

Saní like ice, like winter, like shivers.
Saní:wa: like my heart, like this wind, like the river.
Saní:se: like wet socks, like old tears, like my breath.
Saní:la: like our culture and our language returning from death.

So:ti like a rock, like a mountain, like the Earth.
So:tiwa: like a child, like a womb, like giving birth.
So:tise: like deer sinew, like corn kernels, like our work.
So:tila: like our people, like swift currents, like twisted River Birch.

## Autumn

Prime pumpkins are picked
amongst sweet, moldy leaves
as crisp air turns dark.

## Annual Equinoxes

They sit amongst the Dogwood blooms
as spring fades to summer moons
with warmer days arriving soon:
making plans and planting foods.

They stand amongst the waving grass
watching clouds and hours pass
with sounds of birds as children laugh:
sun drops falling dripped and splashed.

They kneel amongst harvest corn,
watching family walk the rows,
grateful for this life they chose:
reclaiming their ancestral roles.

They lie amongst peaceful dreams
adjacent to icy streams,
next to fire's sacred heat,
surrounded with love and belonging.

## Rotten Apples

Rotten apples,
burning stars
taste so sweet and
take me far
along the glittering rows
of corn pollen tops,
of ancient songs,
of rats and frogs
hopping along the path
of moonbeams.
Laughing amongst
Jack-O-Lanterns
carved by grandma's knife.
Shh! Don't tell a soul
about how you can turn
light switches on and off
with your mind.
Don't tell
how your touch heals the sick
and how your prayers are always heard
like good spells are always cast
with goodwill and faith
in the Divine, in self, and in life.
In that way,
all circles will finish their course
like every snake will eat its tail
for each to belong to its nature,
for love to belong,
and for order to remain for all time.

## Foraging For Hope

Lost, melancholic, and disconnected
I stepped into the backyard to gain some direction.

My mother said her neighbor
would mow down the "weeds"
a day or two later,
but as far as I could see:
wisteria and foxgloves and Witch Hazel leaves,
wild dandelions and daisies
and wild mock berries.

Plants that could cure and could feed
and could soothe us.
Plants from distant lands
and many Indigenous.
Flowing and flourishing
without one human finger lifted
in labor, truly had been gifted
as seeds born directly from
the Earth Mother's womb.
None of them purposeless,
rather unapologetically bloomed.
I sat there in the rain
and ask them their names.
I web-searched their features
while they posed for their pictures.
I thanked them for their medicine
and praised Creator for their existence,
for healing my emotional ails
and for spiritual subsistence.

For though not one of these was plucked
they offered me life: they offered me love.

*"A Prayer to Mani"*

*"Speak Life"*

D. DAYE HUNTER

*"My Native Woman"*

*"Lulu / Lele"*

She is
**AFRO INDIGENOUS**

*"She Is Afro-Indigenous"*
*feat. Shereá D. Burnett, J.D.*
*(Occaneechi Band of the Saponi Nation), Creator of*
*ThisWomansWords, Social Worker, Writer, & Advocate*

*"Bless the Matriarchy"*

# Remembering

In the City That Never Sleeps
lies dormant a piece
of history
that most refuse to see.

They are blinded by racism,
blinded by stereotype,
blinded by violence,
blinded by colonial lies,
blinded by indifference.

They cannot see us
beneath copper or mocha skin,
beneath box braids and soft curls,
beneath broad noses and wide hips,
beneath hip-hop and soul.

Their white, colonial eye
has now caused our own to go blind.
We are blind to our own culture.
We are blind to our own heritage.
We are mute in our own languages.
We are deaf to our own heartbeat
which resounds like ancestral drums.
We've forgotten our own names.
We've forgotten our own grandmothers.
We've forgotten the land.
We've forgotten the dolphins
which once swam upon these shores.

We begin to remember,
and they laugh at us.
We begin to remember,
and our people mock us.

"You are not an 'Indian.'"
"You can't be an 'Indian.'"
"You aren't wearing buckskin or feathers."
"Your skin is too dark; your face is too wide."
"You're just a nigga."

But as painful as it is, at first,
to remember,
remember that you're not alone
for I am remembering, too.


*In honor of the Lenape, Rockaway and Canarsee People and Shinnecock Nation who faced genocide and whose land was stolen to build New York City; and to all the reconnecting urban Native Americans who call the City home.*

# Is It a Crime to Be Afro-Indigenous?

Point of View:
I'm the only Afro-Indigenous person in the room,
but my skin tone is nothing new.
Because I'm half white
mixed with my Black and Native roots,
I "level out" to a slightly light, beige hue.
"She must be from Canada or Oklahoma,"
they think, confessing their thoughts to me later.
My hair pattern is curly but,
"Maybe she just took out her braids" they say.
They mostly welcome me with open arms,
that is until I bring my mom.
She gets the side eye,
with their eyebrows raised.
I will tell you now that I've been invited into racist spaces,
and I mean "INDIGENOUS" racist spaces,
where, when my mother's Blackness
becomes apparent,
everyone gets quiet.
We've gone to photo and video shoots where we are
somehow the only ones who are never included in the final
product.

Most times they assume I am only Native because we are
attending a Native event
and due to my outward appearance.
But how sharply their energies do shift
after I introduce myself as Afro-Indigenous.

Afro-Indigenous peoples,
Black Natives,
we are.
Tokens, scapegoats, and after thoughts
we are not.

I will now let you know
you better check your colonized ideas at MY door.
Laughing about how you don't want to get "too dark" in
the sunlight
or that curly hair is unruly and wild.
I'm tired of the hesitation
in Native people's voices when
mentioning us or our non-Native Black kin
as if our existence is at best uncomfortable,
and at worst a dirty secret, an unspeakable sin.

Then you wonder why we have our own powwows
and crave our own spaces?
Because this bullshit behavior
is putting our lives in danger.
When I first came to Arizona
and connected with Natives out here
I had a growing suspicion
that became a confirmed fear:
that my Blackness would not be and was not welcomed
here.
So, when I introduced myself in the early years
I intentionally excluded that I was Black and Caucasian,
too.
Thankfully, things have changed.
More people started speaking up
and honoring all their ancestral names.
So, I did, too.
But I still carry the scar of denying them.
One day I will have to answer to them.
One day you will have to answer, too.

But today I choose to rise.
Despite the haters and despite
the threat of hate crimes.
Today, I choose to accept myself,

because despite all the people who don't
I deserve it.
I deserve to be seen
and to see myself
as a whole person
outside of colonized, racist notions.
Today, I choose to show my roots
both African and American Indigenous and Caucasian
because our ancestors of light did not see race;
because in this house we honor them
by calling them their rightful names,
and by identifying them as being "enslaved"
not as "slaves."

Today, I choose the youth
who deserve a better future
without aunties who make jokes
behind their backs
about them being Black
or grandmas who, with straight faces,
spew racial slurs and propagate
ideals about not mixing races.

Today, I choose to take up space,
because to be
Afro-Indigenous is,
at its core, to be a human being
and a blessing
and I refuse to deny
the One who created me
Their rightful honor and praise.

## My Native Woman

I'm tired of hearing
"You don't 'look' Native."
I have heard these comments all my life.
Not only directed at me, but at others.
We, of mixed ancestry,
are mislabeled as "Mexican" or "Asian"
by Natives and non-Natives alike.
Native people have a dope sense of humor:
one of the beautiful things about our cultures.
But what is ugly is internalized oppression and negative
self-talk hidden in so called "jokes."

Hey, some of us are Caucasian or Black or Mexican,
mixed with these backgrounds,
and beautifully, awesomely so!
For the record, most Mexican people are Indigenous!
But let's finally stop buying into the stereotype
that "REAL" Natives have long hair.
That "REAL" Natives only have copper skin.
That if we don't fit this ideal, we are somehow less Native
and less valuable to our communities,
to our Mother Earth.

We are all children of Mother Earth.
Each variation,
whether ethnicity, sexual orientation,
background, birthplace, spirituality, or education,
makes us STRONGER not weaker.
There is STRENGTH in diversity.
Our ancestors knew this.
Hence, the establishment of clan systems for identity,
marriage, and child rearing
to ensure genetic diversity.
They also knew the power of cross-cultural exchange.

Not only do these negative stereotypes
separate us as Indigenous peoples,
but they are also the same damaging tropes
that allow things like mascots
and the oversexualization
of Indigenous women
to continue.
Yep, being racist towards me
affects you, too.

Let's put these colorist,
racist ideologies to rest.
A deep skin tone simply means
you've been blessed
and lovingly kissed by the Sun.
Then, there are our sisters
who have been kissed
by the Moon.
Let's embrace long Indigenous hair
which was forcibly cut,
but let us not exclude
those who choose to keep it short.
Let's not forget our relations
who have cut their hair
after a loss of kin.
Let's not shame them
with insinuations or silent judgment.
When appreciating our language and culture,
let's remember those
who have had land and children stolen,
or whose tongue was beaten out of them,
or who lost many ceremonies
in the fire of colonization,
or who had too many grandparents
taken by alcoholism
before they could pass on their traditions.

Let's keep our minds open
to different languages and cultures.
Let's listen before we speak
and understand before we assume.
Our sisters and brothers also have
constellations of freckles,
thick waves,
blonde and red hair,
gray elder eyes
and blue and green ones, too.
Let's decolonize Indigenous phenotypes!

Being Native is not a look:
it's your culture.
It's who you are
and how you identify
with the world around you.
It's your commitment to
learning about your traditions
and honoring the ancestors.
No more pushing one another
down or around.
You are beautiful.
You are sacred.
You are pure magic.
And, most importantly,
your ancestors of light
love you.

## Indigenous AF

Yeah, my hair is kinky and curly,
wavy and thick,
like the buffalo,
and I'm still Indigenous as fuck.

Yeah, my melanin is a deep
copper or mocha,
both grown from this land,
and that's why I'm Indigenous as fuck.

My hair is red or blonde or blue
from boxed products of expression
or from an ancient United Nations or from r*pe,
and I'm still Indigenous as fuck.

My accent is familiar
to pueblos and mountains and reservations,
to New Yorkers; it's Chicanx, it's a Southern drawl,
and I'm still Indigenous as fuck.

My complexion is blessed
with freckles like reflected stars on ocean voyages;
with intentional markings
that tie me to kin and place,
and you better know that I'm Indigenous as fuck.

My prayers are raised high
to the ancestors and divine ones,
to Jesus or to Allah,
and I'm still Indigenous as fuck.

I know how to chop wood and skin deer.
I can't cook for shit, so, I tell stories instead.
I think with my heart, and I feel with my head,

and I'm still Indigenous as fuck.

I honor the old ways,
I adapt to the new,
and none of that shit
makes me less Indigenous than you.

'Cause I'm Indigenous as fuck:
I thought you knew.

## You Don't Own Me

I'm not a damn trophy
for your eyes to wander to in sick lust,
for you to conquer and fuck,
for you to force your touch.

My body was not created for your pleasure.
It was created as a warrior
to protect my spirit,
and to reflect the Divine.

My body is not for you
to rip my spine
over labor of love
or price.

I do not live for your comfort,
to pick you daises or cotton,
to bake you pies with flour
or to bake your mind with flower.
I will not save a seat for your unwavering ego
that would sit beside us as you deny
all that I've taught you,
and all that I've given.
All the while you leave
me no seat for my dignity,
but demand a throne for your pride.
Damn all your trappings
of fragile femininity,
and how I should want
to need you to save me.

Damn the idea that giving up my agency
will make me free
to lounge all day as a kept lady.

Damn the idea that's what
I should want and desire,
because I'm obsessed
with fitting in and standing out:
being nothing by being everything
and being everyone thus being no one.

I'm sick of hating my hair,
and fearing the ticks of a clock
or the passing of a new year
will sap away my power,
because "beauty is the ultimate power
and is an enemy of time."
In this world, ignorant youth is preferred
over wise years and all the answers
to all the questions and "whys"
I asked when I was a child.
We loathe and fear the wild
in us, craving polished toenails
and shaven legs.
Anything overgrown
is viewed as something
to be tamed and conquered.
Sound familiar?

Anything tried and true is old news
and needs to be improved,
because it's "outdated,"
because greed rules this world.
Yet, values and adventure
are the true gems of youth.

I'm tired of hearing you talk
when your words, that they all sing praises of,
I simply cannot relate to anymore.

## Respiration Liberation

You say the air for all is free.
Then why, for us, is it so much harder to breathe?
I'm learning to accept myself
not by contrast of "other,"
but through the roots that come from way back, destroying
the concept of "other."

I'm talking way back
before the "contacts" had a react-
ion to us: the Originals.
Filled with jealousy, it's unbelievable.
This world's favorite words to a Black person's rage are,
"Don't trip," and, "Calm down."
Yet, it trips us up 'til we're lying flat on the ground.
Struggling for air like George, Ahmaud, and Breonna.
Told we're unworthy like Nina, Tony, and Iyonna.
You think 'cause I'm passing, I'm passive?
I'm light skinned, but I ain't down with that shit.

My ancestors' blood of love
runs stronger in my veins
than that of greed and hate.
Stronger than lynching and bullets and r*pe.
Stronger than generations of assimilation and apartheid.
Stronger than 500 years of enslavement and genocide.

I choose to be on the side of justice.
Nah, not "just ice," but truly making wrongs right.
See, I'm here for the people.
You're here for your ego.

We don't need your performative narrations:
we need real change and REPARATIONS!
We need, no, DEMAND

land back for Native nations,
a safe place of refuge for the Afro-diaspora.
We ain't begging abdications no more,
and, frankly, we ain't asking, bruh!

We demand because our babies' lives are at stake.
No more time to be political bait.
We don't need your nationalism,
and false worship of self.
We need to rebuild our communities,
to give and receive help.

To my fellow Black relatives,
all peoples Indigenous,
Migrants seeking refuge,
and those free to be and love who they do.
To human beings
of all backgrounds, nations, colors, and creeds
who teach love from the mountains to the streets:
Red is the color we all bleed,
but ours will continue to spill
until this is a world
where we can all breathe.

# Blooming

Rise dear one
from your slumber.
Widen your eye
and watch with wonder.

Once, you only
knew the Earth.
Now you've entered
a new birth.

Stretch your spine
and shake your leaves.
Lift your stem
and dig in your feet.

Feel your roots
founded in
those before you
and settle in.

This is your home:
take up your space.
This is your story:
tell it with grace.
Once a seedling,
now a sapling.
Once a sapling,
and now it's happening.

You've flowered.
You've come into bloom.
You've gained your crown:
it looks so good on you!

You stand tall
amongst your people.
You outlast their tests,
because you are equal.

You are equal
even to those who are taller.
You are equal
even to those whom you follow.

Each microbe of life
deserves respect,
deserves empathy,
and you? No less.

You'll go through seasons
of abundance and of drought,
but there is no one who
you can't live without.

Except thyself.
Remember this truth:
there is no one like them,
and no one like you.

You'll feel warm days,
and you'll feel ice.
You'll rue your making,
and praise this life.

One day you will
have many rings,
have laughed a thousand times
with that voice that sings.

One day your body

will start to fade,
but with a strong heart
you'll always stay
a guiding spirit
in this forest
that we call life
like the ones before us.
And when your matter
breaks down finally
your death will transform
into another's blooming.

## Oh, Watch How Loki Laughs at Our Shield Walls Now

I walk in a world of chaos,
a world of lies,
a sea of waves and hallucinations.
The Thunder Gods beat their hammers.
They wait to see if we will sink:
we have been treacherous.

I walk in a desert of uncertainty.
I walk amongst the dead
skinned in breathing Earth.
As I walk, I walk with one million ancestors:
those wielding axes, guarding;
those with spears singing war cries;
those in the high country
with fingers on bow strings one atom thin
telling war stories and doing war dances
as they all chant for my protection.

In this crazy world,
in this dual plane,
in this changing place
I walk.
I pull up my bandana
to cover myself
with all the colors
of all the flowers and all the birds.
I adorn myself with prayers and songs.
I fasten myself with love and with prophecy:
it's the last protection that I have left.

## Barking up the Wrong Tree

I'd like to spit a rhyme
'bout what's been on my mind,
but blocking creative flow
is this prick who crossed the line.
Hitting up my inbox like,
"Knock, knock: it's the identity police.
I don't know you, but you know me.
Not directly, you see, but I'm a common theme:
I feel the need and faux authority
to question how you came to be,
and divide your blood into quantities.
Because your phenotype, Indigenous?
It's hard for me to believe."

Hold up a moment please
while I school them all on my identity.
Black as the night is my clan get it right:
warrior queens from Togo-Benin
coming straight from Africa.
Yeah, I'm light skinned, but I'm still a dark nigga.
Blood Black, heart Black, laugh Black, womb Black:
open me up and you'll see that.
I bear the marks and scars
of my ancestors
who were murdered and r*ped.
I feel it when my womb shakes.
Endometriosis, depression, and heart disease diagnoses
point directly to slavery.
They scoff at our Blackness
all while trying to be us.
You can't: we are your mothers, the original peoples.

Yesáh: Afro Saponi at that.
Yeah, our chiefs saw the strength and plight of our African
ancestors and took them right in.
We had no concept of race only concept of place.
They, WE, became one on this Turtle Island
growing corn and tobacco.
Stolen land and stolen people.
Sound familiar?
That's 'cause we are the Indigenous people of Akụ:čuk,
even if our skin and hair look different.
We adapted and evolved: as we all must
'cause this world is falling apart all around us.

So, that's my mama's clans
and yeah, she married a white man: Irish and Polish.
They came dirt poor: no potatoes, no borscht.
Babushka's ma escaped war
by boat when she was 11 with no family
but her sister.
I'm proud to descend from that little girl.

So, you think you know who's real and who's fake?
You think you have the right to interrogate me?
'Cause our blood is less than "pure"?
Nah, it's mixed as fuck and beautiful
as nature intended,
because diversity is Mother Earth's
genetic champion.

## Light Skinned Sista

I'm a light skinned sista,
but my voice is deep and velvety.
Even on the other line
they can peep my ancestry.

I'm a light skinned sista,
but my laughter is like an auntie cackling.
My blunt observations keep people
hollering and scattering.

I'm a light skinned sista,
but my ass is fat.
You can't see it from the front,
but it switches when I walk.

I'm a light skinned sista,
but I'm down for the cause.
No more Black people dying
and stuck behind bars!

I'm a light skinned sista,
but I stand for the people.
I put my faith in Creator,
and speak-up against evil.


I'm a light skinned sista,
but I don't think I'm better than you.
The blacker the berry, the sweeter the juice.
The part that makes you sweet,
makes me sweet, too.

I'm a light skinned sista,
but I don't think I'm smarter than you.

The darker the hue, the deeper the roots.
Both our ancestors were stolen,
and both our spirits are seeking the truth.

I'm a light skinned sista,
but my pineal gland works!
My melanin may be a bit recessive,
but I'm still connected and empathetic.

I'm a light skinned sista,
and I benefit from light skinned privilege.
But don't get it twisted.
I'll call out a white person for using
the n-word with indifference.

I'm a light skinned sista,
and schools give me higher grades.
So, I shout out my more melinated classmates
when the prof tries to give me praise.

I'm a light skinned sista.
So, work gives me a higher pay.
But they look at me in a daze
when I ask who else is getting a raise.

I'm a light skinned sista,
but I don't want to be your light skinned savior.
Or an "exception," or an "outsider"
or an "abomination."

I'm a light skinned sista,
but all I've ever wanted in this big, ol' world
is to be another precious Black girl
among all the other precious Black girls.

I'm a light skinned sista,

but please just call me a sista.
Because all our Earth tones are blessed,
and I'm done justifying shit to ya.

## This One Is for the Women

This one is for all the women who are "too mean,"
who are praised for their strength, then left because they're
"too much," "too wild," too tired, and too jaded to fit into
little boxes called relationships.

This is for the women who lele loudly
in traditional and office spaces:
in court rooms and protests
demanding rights.

This is for the women who are
"too dark" or light skinned,
stereotyped as "exotic,"
who "seem nice,"
but whose low-rolling fire
eventually drive weak ones away
or keep them away in the first place.

This is for the women who keep up thick walls
to stay safe when all they want
is to be vulnerable
and loved.

# Roots

Tresses like rivers.
Strands like veins.
Like arteries to hearts.
Like follicles to my brain.

This one is for the matriarchs
with hair thick like buffalo:
long and wavy or a bouncy Afro.
This one is for those with copper skin
and ageless beauty.

This one is for the children
of two worlds married into one:
for the children of
Africa and Turtle Island
which might as well be names
for Earth's right arm and her belly
from which spawned
the seed of humanity
for us all to spring forth from and enjoy.
So, let's celebrate our diversities
while honoring the roots
of our first human mothers
beautifully blended with aunties of ancient forests.

## Just Like You, Sis

So subtle she is:
He:ną: Mį:no:sá: in all her luminous glory.
Just like you, gida. Just like you, wine:k.

So powerful she is:
He:ną: Mį:no:sá: as she bends the tides to her will.
Just like you, gida. Just like you, wine:k.

So kind she is:
He:ną: Mį:no:sá: using her light to guide our paths.
Just like you, gida. Just like you, wine:k.

So misunderstood she is:
He:ną: Mį:no:sá: blamed for the madness of weak men.
Just like you, gida. Just like you, wine:k.

So loving she is:
He:ną: Mį:no:sá: reminding us we need to feel to heal.
Just like you, gida. Just like you, wine:k.

So, enduring she is:
He:ną: Mį:no:sá: rising and setting through the test of time.
Just like you, gida. Just like you, wine:k.

## Wrapped in Their Love

My home and my hearth
surrounds me from birth
first as a covering as I enter the Earth,
now as a shield, not a symbol of worth.

Heavy, thick, deerskin
is where my story begins
outlining my figure in
wrinkles of four-legged kin.

Flowers encircle my circumference:
bright yellow daisies of endurance,
and deep, red roses of sufferance
rewarding my patience with abundance.

Swaying, soft, strips of ribbon
bordered by fabric of bold, black matter.
Ribbon from blue to beige: a rainbow of satin
like teachings of old ones embedded in patterns.

Passed down from generation to generation.
Blood born or adopted: all equal relations.
Heeding the call of jingle vibrations.
Each step that I take, healing our nations.

## The Three Sisters

She stands
tall and strong,
our sustainer, our protector
in green, bell bottom pants
with a bright yellow sweatshirt.
She's imposing and
shrinks away from no challenge.
Rather, she reaches for the sky
while we gather beneath her.
She shields us
from the harshness of life.
Yet, makes us stronger within
with hard truths and sick burns
she serves with a grin.
She listens and chuckles
as her sisters bicker
as she stretches her arms
around them like leaves
as they both lean on her.
She is Corn Sister.

She leans against her big sis
acting indifferent
in her bronze oversized sweat suit
with palms casually lifted.
Her lackadaisical attitude isn't persistent
as she cracks loose a smile
and her eyes become misted.
She holds her sisters tight in her arms
connecting and keeping them away from harm.
Some may forget her,
hiding under her big sister's leaves,
but she is their glue
wiping rainy tears from their sleeves.

They won't let it show,
But they need her
more than each of them knows.
They trust her.
She is Bean Sister.

She runs to catch up
as she shouts in distress
towards her two older sisters
in her bright yellow striped dress.
She may be small to the naked eye,
but she's tough as they come
and kicks ass as she lies
low near the Earth
keeping out the weeds
and choking thorns of life.
She brings her sisters great joy,
and, yes, sometimes drama and strife.
Even though she's younger
and shorter and smaller,
neither can deny
that they both rely on her.
She is Squash Sister.

Together they grow, sisters since seeds.
For surely where you see one,
another will be.

# Growth

Gums suckle nipples like mountains of love
which graciously offer ample nourishment.
Fresh, soft skin supple and clear
wrapped around tiny organs.

Watched over with vigilance,
showered with affection and favor,
tiny hands feel new textures.
Tiny mouths taste new flavors.

Tasting their way through the world as they go:
small buds on tongues
their first method of exploration.
Eyes drawn so wide they then seal shut for hours
offering coos and cries in lieu of verbal nuance.

Casting eyes skyward in search of the source
of all the lights and pretty colors
which older ones can't seem to see,
but understand them to be angels and ancestors.

-

Legs grown strong from kicking and playing
now grow longer by the day.
Smiles that were once surrounded by soft, supple skin
display signs of maturity like stubble and acne.

The joyful cries of childhood are now replaced
by the silent, sometimes sulking,
moods of adolescence.
Unamused by a mother's love and more interested
in meeting new friends
and spending time with cousins.

What a way to learn of your place in the world:
a juxtaposition between origin and belonging.
Between immaturity and the craving of acceptance,
somewhere between the known and unknown:
your destiny.

Understanding expectations,
grappling with responsibility,
desiring that which has yet to be discovered.
All leading to the discovery of uncharted waters
deep within yourself.

-

Standing tall amongst a sea of strangers
you are your only kin that exists within this space.
Adapting to cultures foreign and frigid,
acquiring the tools needed to stay afloat the riptide.
Being dealt with more harshly than is required
by people who dictate whether you'll eat or starve.
Withstanding trauma to feed your family
and losing yourself in this modern mirage.

Being rerouted by unexpected circumstances
through sorrow and pain while learning priorities.
Realizing your allies by those who stay through the storm
while others retreat to their soft, lonely beds.

Finding your voice amongst the noise of injustice.
Refusing to stay idle when the people need change.
Channeling the power of the ancestors within you. Working
and praying towards better days.

-

Pieces of meat stuck between teeth
that long ago lost their luster.
Muscles once toned wrapped around bone
gather all the strength they can muster.

Lifting yourself up from a favored couch spot
to watch children play through the blind slats.
Noticing one of them came from your own womb
guiding the small one who descended from her own.

Wrinkles curve upward towards aging eyes
as teeny footsteps totter up wooden stairs
through the doorway with dewy hands
pulling timeworn fingers to see the surprise.

Ancient knees finally land
on soft blankets and Earth,
familiar scents of cedar
and summer wafting in the breeze.
Remembering distant days of the past
while watching the future
as she proudly rolls down the driveway
on only two wheels.

## The Secret Society of Seed Keepers

We is children of the Motherland,
ancestors of diasporic kin.
We is the Fon, Yoruba, Adja, Barons.
We is the Ewe, Kabye, Mina, and Kotokoli.
We is Bantus, Semi-Bantus, and Sudanese;
Kongo, Mongo, Luba, and Mangbetu-Azonde.

We hail from the Kingdom of Dahomey,
the Kingdom of Bamoun,
the Kingdom of Kongo.
We come from tropical forests,
grassland, shrubland,
and savannah.
We come from power,
boisterous laughter,
autonomy, liberation,
and sovereignty.

They came from
the mountains,
on boats and
with Bibles.
They sent spies,
told lies, and
strengthened our rivals.
To they own end
they pointed pens
like rifles
on property deeds
and ownership titles.
They stole Black lands
and Black bodies alike
while remorseless and entitled.
They killed our elders,

r*ped our children,
and separated husbands
and wives.

We heard from abroad
of their arrival.
We armed our boys
when they killed our men
without final
goodbyes.
We cried
and cried,
and realized this
was the call for survival.
We scooped up seeds
in our hands splashed with
the tears and sweat of
genocide.
The spirit guides
already previewing
the nearing apartheid.
Late at night
by fire light
we, with shaky hands,
placed these seeds
gently onto our daughters
braided heads:
Amara kale, basil, and black-eyed peas;
cola, cotton, sorrel, and sesame;
melon, tamarind, gourds, and mahonia;
rice, gourds, gold, and okra.
We was dragged onto slaver ships
with these seeds in our hair,
and Seeds in our bellies,
both unseen, praying
they would be carried

a long ways from here.

Days without hope,
nights without end:
in this tragic way
we arrived in Turtle Island.
Many of us died along the way
of hunger, of disease,
or refusing to be called "slave."
We unknowingly travelled from
the ocean to the rivers,
our heads bashed against
ship columns
and 4-foot-high ceilings.
We shakily stepped upon the shore
not knowing the land as we had before.
Not knowing if we'd be separated
from mother or sister.
Losing our babies
to a white man's whimsies.
Each family member removed,
each body part severed,
each dignity stripped,
but our spirits didn't weaken.
We loved our babies as best we could
with a bottle in our hand
in that hell of a pit
they call a plantation
all's the while swinging
and singing and praying
and planting and hiding
these Seeds.
Hundreds of years
we been waiting for justice:
to plant our seeds
without fearing our farms

being taken from us,
to grow the Seed in our belly
with our freedom of choice,
to speak loudly
again and lift up our Voice.
We been watching and
waiting for centuries.
We sent some
of our spirits back down there,
you see,
to push back, to speak up,
to follow or lead,
to rise up, to plant anew,
to fight or to flee.
Now this child before you,
as light as may be,
though her hair is straighter
and can't carry no seed
of okra and melon,
of our rice or our peas,
she carries something
much different, can you see?
Something that
each of our people
now desperately needs.
This Seed is called hope
that we planted within her.
Now, she plants it in you.
May it feed and sustain you
across the rockiest oceans,
and through the darkest
of winters.

## She Is

She is cellulite
and thick thighs,
lean ankles
and eyes on fire,
hair a mess
and strut on fleek.
She is herself, authentically.

She is always
running late,
but on time to graduate.
Asking no permission
from any man or creed,
she enjoys what she wants,
but invests in her needs.
She is whoever the fuck she wants to be.

She listens to sisterly advice,
and stays up praying all night.
Her heart is unconditional,
but she has boundaries.
She slows for no one,
but moves with ease.
She is one with self, one at peace.

## Life Givers

Some life givers
give birth to babies
who become children,
who become adults,
who become mothers, fathers;
who become thinkers, leaders.
Bi:wa. And that is good.

Some life givers
give birth to ideas
which become sketches,
which become rough drafts,
which become nothing then something,
which become messy and beautiful.
Bi:wa. And that is good.

Some life givers
give birth to thoughts
which become rants,
which become speeches,
which become books,
which becomes inspiration.
Bi:wa. And that is good.

Some life givers
give birth to seeds
which become roots,
which become saplings,
which become corn,
which becomes nourishment.
Bi:wa. And that is good.

Some life givers
give birth to hope

which becomes joy,
which becomes happiness,
which becomes dreams,
which becomes healing.
Bi:wa. And that is good.

## Waneni

Bitter winds arrive
blowing snow as we stock meat,
and huddle for warmth.

## Water Justice

A crab is born on July 1st:
my great-grandmother,
the eldest born,
a matriarch.
Water.

A judge is born on October 6th:
my grandmother,
the eldest born,
a matriarch.
Justice.

A fish is born on February 22nd:
my mother,
the eldest born,
a matriarch.
Water.

Another fish is born on March 7th:
my sister,
the eldest born,
a matriarch.
Water.

A judge is born, once again, on October 17th:
my niece,
the eldest born,
a matriarch.
Justice.

"Water
Justice.
Water, Water
Justice."

The ancestors whisper
then shout this anthem
like lines in a poem,
like lyrics in a song
like words in a prayer.
They remind us
that they will have justice
for being forced over
the waters.
They remind us
that they will have justice
for these wrongs.

"Water Justice!
Water, Water Justice!"

## Left Handprints

Left handprints
leave marks on my heart
connected to wrists
that are connected to bangles,
one silver bangle to be exact,
with engraved roses and thorns
that represent bittersweetness.

Left handprints
leave marks on car keys
connected to handles
that are connected to doors,
of right doors to be exact,
never left doors, because left doors
represent freedom and control.

Left handprints
leave marks on paper
connected to testing
which is connected to intelligence,
Western intelligence to be exact,
with scribbled red pen markings
that represent preconceived notions of worth.

Left handprints
leave marks on fabric
connected by thread
that is connected by arithmetic,
stitched arithmetic to be exact,
sewn when no one is watching
which represents pride
and self-approval.

## Jidata'umi

Jidata'umi,
I think about you daily.
What you smelled like.
What your laugh sounded like.
Then I realize: I am your smell,
I am your laughter.
Mama says sometimes
when I'm throwing looks
it scares her,
'cause I look like you
with those deep eyes.
Deep eyes and sad smile.
But I know now that you're smiling wide.
You watch over me every day
with love and fierce devotion.
You consult with the powers that be:
they made you and they made me.
You passed a few months before we,
the next generation, were born.
But I lay within my mother's womb
whilst she lay within yours.

Jidata'umi,
we have a connection
that spans thousands of generations
of Black girl magic, of Black queens,
and of Black womanhood.
Your life taught me this,
"Life ain't gonna be easy baby,
but God will get you through it."
I hear it as if those exact words left your lips.
All I have left of you is a couple of photos, stories,
and genetically inspired remembering's.
I remember how the trauma, the lynching,

the booze, and the sadness tried to drown you.
I play it back in my DNA memory
like an old-time movie.
I sit with you as we watch.
You squeeze my hand and cry a little tear.
I wipe it away and you smile wide again.
"It's gonna be okay, grandmama.
I'll do my best to ease your pain with the beauty of my life.
In healing myself I know I will heal you, too."

Jidata'umi, beautiful Black queen
sitting in delicate lace,
adorned with roses,
and surrounded by lady bugs.
One day I will sit in the presence of your power.
Until then: I embody it.

## No More

The British soldier come and say,
"This ain't your land.
This ain't your land.
This ain't your land no more."

The Sunday preacher come and say,
"These ain't your Gods.
These ain't your Gods.
These ain't your Gods no more."

The schoolmarm come and say,
"These ain't your words.
These ain't your words.
These ain't your words no more."

The white settler come and say,
"This ain't your maize.
This ain't your maize.
This ain't your maize no more."

The grandparents stand and say,
"We ain't your 'slaves.'
We ain't your 'slaves.'
We ain't your 'slaves' no more!"

The mamas and papas stand and say,
"These ain't our ways.
These ain't our ways.
These ain't our ways no more!"

The children stand and say,
"We ain't afraid.
We ain't afraid.
We ain't afraid no more!"

The seeds lie in wait and say,
"We will remain.
We will remain.
We will remain forever more!"

## It's Pronounced, "Afro-Indigenous"

They said we were "Negroes."
They said we were "Mongrels."
We said, "It's pronounced, 'Afro-Indigenous.'"

They said we were "mixed breeds."
They said we were "abominations."
We said, "It's pronounced, 'Afro-Indigenous.'"

They said we were fakes.
They said we were delusional.
We said, "It's pronounced, 'Afro-Indigenous.'"

They said we were "just niggas."
They said we were extinct.
We said, "It's pronounced, 'Afro-Indigenous.'"

## Mother's Daughter

Yeah, they say I'm "crazy",
but my friends seem to like me better that way.
All those who've called me baby:
Ooo, they know I'm some type of way,
and I ain't gone stop 'til I've made my way.

'Cause I'm my mama's daughter.
She gets it from her mother.
I come from tears and laughter.
I come from mud and water.

I seem to defy definition.
By the book "norm" was never my potion.
It was more corn whiskey than moonshine
and wood that kept us warm those nights.

'Cause I'm my mama's daughter.
She gets it from her father.
I come from tears and laughter.
I come from mud and water.

Ain't no police pushin'
up on us backwoods Black NDN's.
If you any less than God
and mess with us you'll be looking
down the barrel of a shotgun.
'Cause I'm my mama's daughter.
She gets it from her grandfather.
It's what the backwoods foster.
Don't let us sneak up on ya!

## Cut From the Same Cloth

We're cut from the same cloth, gida,
descendants of the same DNA.
You and I, gida,
are so different,
but are one and the same.

Born from earth and water.
Born of air and flame.
You and I, gida,
are so different,
but are one and the same.

Raised amongst Cedar trees.
Raised amongst tall buildings.
You and I, gida,
are so different,
but are one and the same.

Skin kissed by sun rays.
Skin kissed by moonlit rain.
You and I, gida,
are so different,
but are still one and the same.

## Healing Rain

The pull of wind, the pull of chain.
Let healing rain, let healing rain,
let healing rain ease your pain.

The size of hills, the size of grain.
Let healing rain, let healing rain,
let healing rain ease your pain.

From deep within, in heart and brain.
Let healing rain, let healing rain,
let healing rain ease your pain.

The sun shines bright, the darkness fades.
Let healing rain, let healing rain,
let healing rain ease your pain.

Our grief will pass, our joy: regained.
Let healing rain, let healing rain,
let healing rain ease your pain.

# I Am Born Of

I am born of early mornings,
of sitting on porches with shotguns,
of sipping on coffee and herbal teas,
of watching cardinals and blue jays
prepare for their day.

I am born of thunderstorms,
of loud thunder and dry lightning,
of sun showers all the same,
of visiting gentle rain
which lounges then falls from swollen clouds.

I am born of humidity,
of heavy air and the smell of mulch,
of cicadas and thick, frizzy hair,
of skin and lungs being nourished by moisture.

I am born of laughter,
of joy which comes with sun rise,
of healing wounds of unkind pride,
of remembering worth,
and why I rose in the first place.

## Written Medicine

Written medicine is fickle yet sure.
I sit in silence wondering if the words have gone for good
like one lies under the cold stars wondering
if the winter Sun will ever rise again;
like one sits in their grief wondering
if they'll ever feel joy again.
Then, it happens suddenly
like planted corn sprouts overnight,
like babies grow before your eyes.

Like planting corn and like growing babies,
written medicine comes with contractions
and growing pains.

Like planting corn and like growing babies,
written medicine creates more than words on pages,
food in mouths, and mouths that create their own
spoken and written medicine.

Like all these, written medicine
multiplies and creates life of its own,
because written medicine isn't fickle.
It's simply for the patient,
and it's always worth waiting for.

## Reparations

Reparations aren't only monetary.
They are the legal ability to relearn our languages.
They are the decency to express our cultures
without ridicule.

Reparations aren't only monetary.
They are resources that money
alone can't buy like lost relatives
and clean water and heritage seeds.
It's having access to sacred places
not devastated by greed.

Reparations aren't only monetary.
They are the mending of our hearts,
and the rekindling of kinship,
and the reconnecting of relatives
both winged and two and four-legged.

Reparations aren't only monetary.
But it sure as hell includes money:
the cheapest of all currency,
the weakest of all power,
the worst symbol of value,
but needed, nonetheless, in this
pre-revolutionized, pre-Indigenized world.

## Bless the Matriarchy

My womb retched.
I fell to my knees in pain.
I was not in labor. No.
I was trapped in a cycle of imbalanced hormones,
and false labor, the constant state of which
threatened my life
and the life of my own children to come.
I crawled outside towards my front porch.
I then noticed I was not alone.
There was a creature, a small bee,
crawling there along beside me.
Many times, I saw bees crawling and dying as I walked by.
"Does anyone else see this?"
I often wondered,
tears coming to my eyes.
I asked and most had not.
There, crawling amongst the gravel and cement,
I realized: the bee and I are one in the same.
Life givers:
he the pollinator, directed by his queen and
I, the Earth where the pollen grew
and became a flower and food.
I realized that these pesticides,
chemicals, resource extractions,
and failed attempts to tame
and overthrow Mother Earth
were beating down on our bodies
like war tanks on soft Earth,
like drills piercing sacred mountain tops.
It was then that I saw that our futures were inextricably
linked:
to save our wombs we must save the bees.
In saving you, I save me.

## She Is Afro-Indigenous

She stands tall
amongst cedar trees, amongst her ancestors
who stand on the Ivory Coast,
and amongst her ancestors
who stand on Carolina river shores.
Her skin shines ebony as she stands there,
hand in hand with the Moon,
as tides come in and bow at their collective power,
bowing with fin and claw.
She is Yesáh. She is Afro-Indigenous.

She stands firm
in the truth her people ache for
during court proceedings
advocating against domestic violence,
and during lectures teaching students
how to elevate their voices.
She uses her fierce fire
and unquenchable thirst for justice
while writing late nights
and transmuting her own experiences.
She is Yesáh. She is Afro-Indigenous.

*The second stanza is dedicated to Shereá D. Burnett, J.D. who is Afro-Indigenous, a proud citizen of the Occaneechi Band of the Saponi Nation, and the Creator of ThisWomansWords.*

# Mu:nti

The curved outline of her paws,
the dexterity of her claws,
the gentle power of her jaws,
the soft trill of her calls.

Her eyes which convey a million words
of the wisdom of roots and herbs
speaking life into millions of forms,
warning of the darkest storms.

Her heart for young ones
wielding fierce protection,
yielding milk and nutrition,
shielding from harm and rejection.

Her mind to explore all the galaxies
to teach truth and bring light to fallacies;
to bring depth and reconcile families;
to sooth casualties and embrace "abnormalities."

Her skin to keep warm:
herself, her cubs, and humans
who honor her life once she's gone,
because she protects us from the cold.

Her fat to keep healthy,
to fuel herself and feed babies,
to make grease for Saponi
against sunburn and skin cracking.

Her digging produces medicine,
embracing masculine and feminine,
to add marrow to skeleton,
to pass down healing regimens.

Her legs to climb cedars,
to birth and carry leaders
as tincture makers and keepers,
to cure sadness and fevers.

Her prints in the dirt
to remind us we walk the Earth
not as lenders, but as borrowers
as we humbly walk beside her.

## North Carolina

North Carolina,
you are home to many things:
millions of trees,
histories worth thousands of centuries,
red mud and red earth
that, when exposed,
shine like tree bark.

You are home to
the resilient songs we sing,
and, also,
to genocide and enslavement.

You are home to
Yesáh: Saponi, Occaneechi,
Meherrin, Waccamaw-Siouan,
Lumbee, Coharie, and Cherokee.
You are home to descendants from
Guinea, Mali, Niger, and Nigeria;
Ghana, Togo, Benin, and Congo;
Cameroon, Senegal, Liberia, and Gambia.

You are home to Black Croatan Congressman Hiram
Rebels.
Home to the man once enslaved who became
a lawyer, the Congressman from Lumberton:
George Henry White.
Home to Warriors who ran out the klan.
Home to Ulali,
and the first Black Indian's powwow

North Carolina,
you are home to many things.
Most importantly,

you are home to family,
you are home to ancestors,
you are home to me.

## Ati:

Home:
where there are gardens in the backyard,
wells in the side yard,
fishing poles on the back porch,
and shotguns by the front door:
home.

Home:
where deer roam and bears climb,
where elders laugh and ancestors lie:
home.

Home:
Where everyone looks like me,
walks like me, and talks like me.
Where we speak without words
and understand without seeing:
home.

Home:
where oakwood becomes four walls.
Oh, if they could talk, they'd say it all:
home.
I'm talking about home.


Home:
where summer mossy green
turns to sweet, moldy leaves,
where icy rivers turn to Dogwoods blooming:
home.
Home.

Home:

where family will always be
and where I always want to be.
Though I may roam, I'll always return here:
back at home,
back at home.

## Back at Home

Walking softly
through the piney
woods on soft snow
as cold winds blow,
and then we'll go:

Back at home.
Back at home.
Back at home.
Back at home.

Growing a family
from seeds to a tree;
water flowing
as flowers are blooming,
and then we'll be:

Back at home.
Back at home.
Back at home.
Back at home.

# I Am

I am a child of the Divine.
I am from the place where the Earth meets the Sky.
I am woman,
I am life.
I am the wind in the trees,
I am the leaves on the breeze.
I am the massive body of celestial kings and queens.
I am words on messengers' wings.
I am truth and I am light.
I am the holy and the sacred ones.
I am their daughter.
I am all my relations.
I am life.

I am Yesáh.
I am Mother Buffalo's child.
I am the milk that she feeds her calf.
I am its footprints in the snow.
I am the warmth in her skin
that has warmed our people
for a thousand generations.
I am smoke lines of prayer
that rise from rooftops into the cold night air.
I am stories woven into the rings of ancient trees.
I am water that channels through the Earth
and the life it brings.
I am the destiny of an eternal legacy.

I am the swaddled babe
in Grandmother Bear's paws.
I am the leader demonstrating the strength
held within her claws.
I am the late-night stories
of grandfathers past.

I am my mother's love.
I am my grandmother's laugh.
I am the courage of the man
who uses the strength of his hands to feed his clan.
I am the war paint splashed across
my grandfather's face.
I am a protector's honor and a warrior's fate.
I am family.

I am the strength of my great-grandmothers:
a great-grandmother who fled the potato famine and a
great-grandmother who escaped Nazi invasion;
a great-grandmother who watched her people fall to
the Earth as they watched the stars fall from the sky
buried under the rubble of the forgotten universe;
and a great-grandmother who kept her feet in the mud, legs
crippled and twisted as they bent underneath the weight of
a thousand lashings.
I am the endurance in her knees as they gave way,
but her heart never swayed
even as hands smeared in the blood of her ancestors
drove crimson whips deeper,
and deeper into her ebony flesh.
She cried out.
But even as she fell, she stood for her people.
I am the hope she found at the bottom
of a northern-bound mule wagon.
She is not a victim.
She won't let them defeat her.

I am the hopes, dreams, and aspirations
of a woman far beyond her space and time.
I am her kind heart and endless imagination.
I am her survival and her determination.
I am the spirit within her
hidden for many winters,

and at last revealed as she stepped
into the beautiful, blooming dawn of a new life.
I am raw power reawakened.
I am reincarnated.
Mima he:ną́:. I am my mother.

I am gray matter.
I am a new beginning.
I am determined.
I am returning.
I am life.

# Glossary

## Yesáh or Tutelo Saponi Language

aka:tʰeka = hot

Akụ:čuk = the High Plains of northern North Carolina and southern Virginia; the territory of Yesáh (Saponi) people after their migration from the Ohio River Valley many centuries before colonization.

ati: = home

Á:tʰi Mạ:tǫ́: = Father Sky

bisé:huk = thank you all (emphatic)

bi:wa = it is good, thank you (observation)

gida = cousin

he:nạ́: = mother (first person)

He:nạ́: Mị:no:sá: = Mother Moon

kihó: = come here

mahé: = woman

maní = water

mima = I am

Mị: Sun

mu:nti = American Black Bear

saní = cold

so:ti = strong

wasu:ti = mind

wine:k = sister

yạ:di = heart

Yesáh = The People (Eastern Siouan)

## O'odham Language

O'odham jeved: O'odham land

# References

Katz, W. L. (2012). *Black Indians: A hidden heritage*. Atheneum Books for Young Readers.

# Resources

**Adult Children of Alcoholics and Dysfunctional Families**
310-534-1815
www.adultchildren.org

**Al-Anon Family Groups**
1-888-425-2666
www.al-anon.org

**Alcoholics Anonymous**
1-800-839-1686
www.aa.org

**Endo Black Incorporated**
202-918-3418
www.endoblack.org

**Fibromyalgia Support for Women**
202-918-3418
www.fibrowomen.com

**Narcotics Anonymous**
1-818-773-9999
www.na.org

**National Domestic Violence Hotline**
1-800-799-SAFE (7233)
www.thehotline.org

**National Indigenous Women's Resource Center**
406-477-3896
www.niwrc.org

**National Suicide Prevention Hotline**
1-800-273-8255
www.suicidepreventionlifeline.org

**Native Land**
www.native-land.ca